For the voices once overlooked—and the hearts that now listen —A.P.

In memory of Andrew Melvin Brown Sr.

And to Dr. Elizabeth Claytor, the librarian who was a hero to me in middle school —D.R.

The New York Times

HIDDEN HEROES

Ten Overlooked Trailblazers

Written by Amisha Padnani
Illustrated by Dominique Ramsey

Crown Books for Young Readers New York

Crown Books for Young Readers
An imprint of Random House Children's Books
A division of Penguin Random House LLC
1745 Broadway, New York, NY 10019
penguinrandomhouse.com
rhcbooks.com

Based on *Overlooked* by Amisha Padnani and The New York Times, published in 2023 by Ten Speed Press, an imprint of the Crown Publishing Group, a division of Penguin Random House LLC.

Photography credits: Bessie Coleman: George Rinhart/Corbis, via Getty Images; Annie Edson Taylor: Pictorial Press Ltd./Alamy; Miki Gorman: United Press International; Joe Capers: courtesy of the family of Joe Capers; Molly Nelson: Everett Collection; Sanmao: Huang Chen Tien Hsin, Chen Sheng, and Chen Chieh through Crown Publishing Company Ltd.; Ruby Payne-Scott: Fiona Hall; Ralph Lazo: Japanese American National Museum, gift of Rose Hanawa Tanaka; Lorenza Böttner: Leslie-Lohman Museum of Art; Usha Mehta: Reuters.

Editor: Kelly Delaney
Designer: Véronique Lefèvre Sweet
Copy Editors: Patricia Callahan and Jenny Golub
Managing Editor: Tisha Paul
Production Manager: Claribel Vasquez

Library of Congress Cataloging-in-Publication Data is available upon request.
ISBN 978-0-593-42628-9 (trade) — ISBN 978-0-593-42629-6 (lib. bdg.) — ISBN 978-0-593-42630-2 (ebook)

The text of this book is set in 13-point ITC Legacy Serif Pro Medium Condensed.
The illustrations were created using Procreate and Photoshop.

Manufactured in China
10 9 8 7 6 5 4 3 2 1

The authorized representative in the EU for product safety and compliance is Penguin Random House Ireland, Morrison Chambers, 32 Nassau Street, Dublin D02 YH68, Ireland, https://eu-contact.penguin.ie.

When I was in school, I learned about heroes in history, people like Abraham Lincoln, George Washington, and Albert Einstein. But where were the people who looked like me? Weren't any of them heroes, too?

I grew up to become a journalist and began working at a newspaper that publishes obituaries about famous people. Obituaries are stories about important people who did amazing things, like doctors who saved people's lives or actors who made our favorite television shows. We write obituaries when people die to make sure their lives are remembered.

But when I looked at the pictures of these people, I had the same question: Why were they mostly white men? Where were the women? Where were the people who came from other parts of the world? Weren't they important, too?

I decided to look for them, and I learned that there were *many* people who did incredible things but were not memorialized. These people had big imaginations—*so* big that they were TOO BIG for history! But it's important that we celebrate them. They showed us a lot about the world, and in learning their stories, we will better understand our history.

Bessie Coleman

VROOOOOMMM!

Bessie Coleman's plane was so loud she could barely hear the audience cheering below. She yanked on the controls. Her plane flipped upside down. NOW she could hear them. They were chanting her name!

Bes-SIE!

She flipped right side up again.

Bes-SIE!

She got out and stood on the top wing of the plane.

Bes-SIE! Bes-SIE! Bes-SIE!

Bessie sure did have an exciting life. But it wasn't easy.

Ever since she was little, Bessie had been told what she could do—and what she could *not* do. She could *not* be a pilot, even though it was her dream.

Bessie was born on January 26, 1892, when Black people in the United States were not treated equally to white people. They had to use separate bathrooms, ride separate buses, shop at separate stores, and attend separate schools. No Black woman had ever been allowed to become a pilot, but it was all Bessie wanted.

Bessie wouldn't take no for an answer. France was more welcoming to Black women, so she traveled all the way across the Atlantic Ocean and joined a flight school there. When she returned home in 1921, she broke another barrier—in the sky. She was the first Black woman pilot in America! And everyone wanted to see her fly.

Bessie showed people how to soar beyond their limits.

Bessie Coleman Timeline

- January 26, 1892: Bessie is born in Atlanta, Texas. She has twelve brothers and sisters.
- 1898: Bessie walks four miles to school every day, where often the students are given no paper or pencils.
- 1903: Orville and Wilbur Wright make history with their first flight.
- 1910: Bessie attends college in Oklahoma but runs out of money and has to quit.
- 1915: Bessie goes to a beauty school and gets a job at a salon in Chicago.
- 1919: Bessie's brother returns from World War I and tells her about women flying planes in France. Bessie decides to go to a school in France to learn to fly.
- 1921: She graduates with her pilot's license and returns to the United States.
- 1922–1926: She dazzles audiences with her air shows around the country. Everyone calls her Queen Bess.
- April 30, 1926: In a horrific accident, her plane suddenly stops working while in the air. Bessie dies in the crash. More than ten thousand people come to her funeral to say farewell.

Annie Edson Taylor

A powerful river roars toward a cliff. When the water reaches the edge, it crashes down 160 feet, as tall as a building or twenty grizzly bears balancing on each other's heads.

This is the waterfall at Niagara, on the border of the United States and Canada. It is a roller coaster in nature, and Annie Edson Taylor is about to ride on it—inside a barrel. Many people have tried the feat before. None have succeeded.

Annie Edson Taylor was born on October 24, 1838. She worked as a teacher but wanted to be rich and famous. She hoped her barrel adventure could get her there.

One afternoon in October 1901, she climbed inside, sealed herself in with a wall of pillows, and braced herself for the ride of her life. The barrel sailed down the river, swooping and swerving. A crowd oohed and aahed in suspense as the barrel swung into the air. Then it soared down, swirling and swishing. Annie swayed and spun about, trying not to get seasick. She could not *wait* for this ride to be over. Finally, a team of boatmen tore the lid off the barrel. There was Annie, bruised and startled, with a gash on her forehead.

"Good God!" said one of the rescuers. "She's alive!"

Annie had done it! She showed the world what courage looks like.

The First Man Over Niagara

Annie was the first person to go over Niagara Falls and survive. Ten years later, the first *man* to make the plunge was Bobby Leach. He was a stuntman and swimmer who did diving tricks for Barnum & Bailey Circus. He also jumped out of big balloons in the sky using a parachute.

Bobby owned a restaurant near the falls. He told his customers that anything Annie could do, he could do better. He built a barrel made of steel, and in 1911 he made the treacherous tumble. A crowd watched from the top of the falls, and more people waited at the bottom. As the barrel tumbled toward the edge, everyone was silent. After the barrel made its bumpy descent, a man used a hammer to open it. Bobby was in bad shape, with two broken legs and a broken jaw, but he was alive. The crowd at the bottom cheered! The people at the top heard the cheers, and they knew Bobby had done it. Bobby spent six months in the hospital recovering.

Miki Gorman

Miki Gorman was so hungry. She ordered not one but *two* huge plates of food, piled high with eggs, mushrooms, and spinach. Miki was tiny. Could she eat all that?

Well, she needed the energy. "I'm running the New York City Marathon tomorrow!" she exclaimed. "And I'm going to win."

Miki was born on August 9, 1935, to Japanese parents in China. There had been very little to eat when she was a kid. Miki was *always hungry*. She was embarrassed by how small she was.

She moved to the United States, where, one day, she went to a gym so she could become bigger and stronger. She saw people running on a track. Running was such fun! The wind blew through her hair as her legs moved like wheels.

She trained very hard for the New York City Marathon. She ran around the track thousands of times. She sped up and down tall hills. Even when it was pouring rain, she yanked herself out of bed to go for a run.

At the starting line, an official fired a gun. It was time to go! This was no easy race. At one point, she ran over a big bridge, and the hard metal hurt her feet. Then a big dog jumped up to lick her! *Then* there was a gust of wind so fierce that she hid behind the taller runners.

At last, she could see the finish line. As she ran through it, she learned she was the first woman to get there. She won! "I finally realized that being small didn't have to hold me back," she said, sighing with relief.

Miki showed the world that determination can get you places.

More About Marathons

A marathon is a very long race that many people run at the same time while crowds cheer them on. The name "marathon" comes from the city of Marathon in ancient Greece. There was a battle in Marathon between two armies, the Persians and the Athenians. As the story goes, when the Athenians won, they sent a runner named Pheidippides to Athens to spread the good news. It was a long way—about 25 miles—and Pheidippides was very tired. Today a marathon is a bit longer—26.2 miles. It was extended in 1908 in London so that the children of the royal family could watch from their castle.

Marathons are hard, and runners train for months before competing. They are held all over the world, with the biggest ones being the New York City Marathon and the Boston Marathon (both of which Miki won twice). There was a time when women were not allowed to compete in marathons. People thought women were too weak. But in 1967, Kathrine Switzer signed up for Boston with her initials, "KS"—the race organizers figured she was a man—and finished the race. Now about half of the people who run New York City and Boston are women.

300

Joe Capers

Joe Capers could hear even the smallest sound. If a mouse were to whisper, chances were Joe could hear it.

But Joe could not see. He was always walking in the dark. He never felt alone, though. That's because he could hear music in his head wherever he went. *Ba bump, ba boom, ba bump, ba boom,* the steady rhythm of hip-hop. Music was his life. He also had a guide dog named Tenor who never left his side.

Joe was born on November 6, 1957. He lost his eyesight when he was eight. When he grew up, he built a recording studio in his basement. It was very crowded: There were computers and knobs and switches and microphones and speakers! He was a music producer, and his job was to help other musicians make their songs sound good.

He especially loved hip-hop. In the 1980s, hip-hop was a new culture, with special dance moves and clothing. Hip-hop helped Black artists like Joe feel free to express themselves. He helped many musicians become famous. When people came to Joe to make their music, he had one rule: They had to memorize the words of their songs. One time he heard someone rustling their papers. "I'm blind! I ain't deaf!" he yelled. Everyone started laughing.

Joe showed the world that people don't need eyesight to have a vision.

Oakland Stroke

One of the famous musical acts that Joe helped was Tony! Toni! Toné! Here are some of the words from their song "Oakland Stroke":

Individually picking out the brothers that jam
Commonly known are people like Sly and Graham
Something kinda special about the grooves they wrote
They all had the flavor of the Oakland Stroke
That's the bass drum kickin', the high-hat lickin'
A groove so hard it makes your feet kickin'
To a dope groove, I mean, a fresh groove
It's a guaranteed hit to make your body move
Others try to hang but they just can't cope
They must come to realize, it's the Oakland Stroke

Molly Nelson

Thump-tha-thump-tha-thump-tha-thump. The drumbeats echoed through the trees.

Deep in Maine, where the river flowed through the forest, there was a little Native American girl who loved to dance. Her name was Molly Nelson. And her tribe was called the Penobscot. The Penobscot loved music, nature, and colors as bright as the sky.

Molly was born on November 17, 1903, and began dancing when she was little. Her long braids bounced when her moccasins *tippity tap tapped* the ground in hops and skips.

When she was older, she left the forest to dance for different crowds—crowds that had never met Native American people before. They thought her dancing was strange. They made fun of her, and she felt like she didn't belong.

But Molly didn't change the way she danced. She wanted the world to know about her culture. She decided to perform in France, where she found a more welcoming audience. There, people wanted to know *more* about the Penobscot; they didn't try to change her.

Molly Nelson taught the world the importance of being yourself.

More About the Penobscot People

- Penobscot comes from the word "penawapskewi" in the Algonquian language. It means "rocky ledges," referring to the rocky riverbeds in their homeland.
- They mostly live in Maine. In Molly's day, they relied on the Penobscot River for food, like fish and wild berries, and lived in wigwams, which are cone-shaped houses made from tree bark. But today they live in houses and apartments.
- When Molly was alive, they wore clothing made from animals, like deerskin, which they decorated with colorful beads and designs.
- They built canoes to travel along the water and trade materials with other people. They also created pottery and baskets.
- Their rich culture involves a tradition of telling stories to each other about animals and nature. Usually, nothing is written down—instead, they tell the stories from memory.

Sanmao

When Sanmao was little, she told her teacher that she wanted to become a garbage collector so she could roam the streets for treasures. The teacher scolded her for being silly.

Sanmao (pronounced san-MOW) didn't become a garbage collector. And she didn't roam the streets. She roamed the *world*, and she wrote stories about her many adventures. One of her favorite places was the Sahara, a big sandy desert in Africa, like a beach that stretches on forever. During the day, the sun shines bright, making the sand warm and soft like a pillow. At night, the sky twinkles with millions of stars. Sanmao slept outside, and it was like a beautiful dreamland. In the Sahara, she saw goats and camels and made many friends. She lived in a gray house with a hole in the wall and a light bulb hanging from the ceiling. It was very ugly, but she didn't mind. For her, this life was like "a fantasy," she wrote.

Sanmao was born on March 26, 1943, in China. Growing up, she was very curious and read a lot of books. She enjoyed losing herself in other people's stories. She had a vivid imagination. When she first arrived in the Sahara desert, she wrote: "I looked around at the boundless sand across which the wind wailed, the sky high above, the landscape majestic and calm." When people read her stories, they felt like they were standing next to her. They called her the "wandering writer."

Sanmao showed people how to find beauty everywhere they look.

Sanmao's Lasting Legacy

Most children dream of who they want to be—an astronaut, a doctor, a teacher. But for many years in China, young girls were expected to get married, have children, and stay with their families. They weren't allowed to do anything else.

So when Sanmao told her friends that she was going to become a world traveler, they laughed. They thought she was joking!

Not only did she follow her dream, but she also wrote about her trips in books and poems.

Sanmao is no longer alive, but her words are. And they still inspire young girls in China who have big dreams. They can be free like Sanmao. They can be *anything* they want.

Ruby Payne-Scott

Did you know that the sun makes sounds? As it sends energy into space, it wiggles, making vibration noises like the ringing of a bell. We're just too far away to hear it.

Ruby Payne-Scott was one of the first people to ever hear the sun. She was a scientist who worked in a lab during World War II. Her job was to build a gadget that could listen for enemy planes. Then she heard something else. It almost sounded like the BOOM of thunder or the ROAR of the ocean. But it wasn't either of those things. It was the sun!

Ruby was born on May 28, 1912, in Australia. She was interested in science as a child, and when she grew up, she got her dream job working in a lab. She fell in love and wanted to get married, but her boss told her that if she did, she would have to leave her job. Ruby didn't want to choose. She wanted to do both. Her friends in the lab didn't want her to leave, either. So she got married, and her friends kept it a secret from their boss. She even hid her wedding ring by wearing it on a necklace instead of on her finger.

Over time, she realized that the sun affected the weather on Earth by creating patterns in heat or wind, leading to clouds or rainfall.

Ruby uncovered mysteries about our universe.

What Is Radio Astronomy?

Ruby helped create a field of science called radio astronomy. Just as we listen to music, these scientists listen for radio waves. They use machines that are like giant ears that can hear invisible signals far, far away. They can hear stars, galaxies, and even exploding stars called supernovas.

Radio astronomy is important because we cannot see everything, even with the best telescopes. Sometimes there are dust clouds in the way, or an object is too dark. By listening, scientists can figure out how hot or cold something is or how fast it's moving. They can map celestial objects and learn when a new star is born and when it dies. They might even be able to detect aliens on other planets.

Space is like a puzzle, and radio astronomers are finding new pieces all the time.

Ralph Lazo

Ralph Lazo was a brave and kind boy, born on November 3, 1924, in Los Angeles, California, near the neighborhood called Little Tokyo.

In the 1940s, during World War II, the United States government sent Americans of Japanese ancestry to camps. These were not fun summer camps. They were more like prisons, with tall fences everywhere. The houses were dirty, and the food was gross. A lot of people became sick. No one was allowed to leave. But unlike those imprisoned for crimes, the people sent to these camps did not do anything wrong. The United States was at war with Japan, and it was punishing people whose families were from Japan. It didn't even matter if those people had been born in the United States.

Ralph was not Japanese, but his friends were. He was Mexican American. At age seventeen, when he learned where his friends were going, he went with them, even though he didn't have to. In the camps, he tried to cheer up his friends by singing songs and playing fun games. When the war was over, everyone was sent back home. But people had spent years in those horrible camps, and thinking about it made them sad. How could they feel safe in their country again?

Ralph was angry about this. He spent the rest of his life making sure that everyone was treated the same way. To him, it didn't matter what their background was. Many people, including Ralph, told the government to apologize to Japanese people, and eventually it did.

Ralph taught people to stand up for what they believe in.

A Day in the Life of an Internment Camp

Living in an internment camp was like living in jail. Every morning an alarm sounded to wake everyone up at the same time. Guards came and took attendance. Families lived in barracks, which were small buildings cramped with a lot of people, and usually there was no running water. Everyone ate their meals together in a huge cafeteria, but there was very little food and they were still hungry.

The adults went to work, cooking and cleaning, while the children went to school. There were activities like sports and arts and crafts, but the camps were surrounded by tall fences, and no one was allowed to leave. There was usually no doctor, so when one person became sick, it wasn't long before *everyone* became sick. In the wintertime it was very cold, and there was no heat. In the summertime it was hot, and there was no air-conditioning. At the end of each day, the guards took attendance again to make sure no one had tried to escape. Everyone went to sleep at the same time, usually on an uncomfortable thin bed or a mat. That is what camp life was like, beginning in 1942; the last of these camps closed in March 1946.

Lorenza Böttner

Lorenza Böttner had a terrible accident when she was nine years old.

She very much wanted a baby bird as a pet, so she climbed a utility tower near her house to find a nest. The mother bird stretched her wings, startling Lorenza, who started to fall and grabbed on to the tower's electrical wires for balance. Lorenza didn't know that the wires were dangerous. Both of her arms were burned, and doctors had to remove them.

At first, Lorenza was sad. She loved to dance and make art. What would she do now? Lorenza put on some music and placed a blank canvas on the ground. She grabbed a crayon between her toes and began drawing lively streaks of color. She took breaks to dance around the room. She called this "dance painting."

Lorenza was born on March 6, 1959, in Chile and later moved to Germany. She was born a boy, but she felt like she should be a girl. She loved to wear her mother's dresses. She decided she could be whatever she wanted.

After her accident, she learned to do everything with her feet and teeth. She used her toes to turn on the sink, brush her hair, and even scratch an itch. To remove her sweater, she used her teeth to lift the collar, then grabbed it with her toes and yanked it over her head.

She often painted herself as a body with a lot of curves and shapes but no arms. Did a person need arms to be beautiful? No. In one painting, she drew herself three times: the first as a woman with long hair, the second as a man with a beard, and the third as a man wearing a suit. Which one *was* she? The answer was all three.

Lorenza showed the world that there is beauty in every one of us.

Bessie Blount

Lorenza wasn't the only person to use her feet instead of her hands. When Bessie Blount was seven years old, her schoolteacher hit her knuckles. When the teacher told her what she had done wrong, she couldn't believe it. "For writing with my left hand!" Bessie exclaimed. Bessie was taught that using your left hand was not considered ladylike. But rather than use her right hand, she taught herself to write with her teeth and her feet.

Many years later, Bessie became a nurse in a hospital during World War II. People who had been injured in the war and lost their arms were coming to the hospital, so Bessie taught them to write with their teeth and their feet. A doctor told her that if she really wanted to help, she should teach these soldiers how to feed themselves. "I'll do that, too!" she replied.

Bessie stayed up many nights building a machine with a tube. When a person bit the tube, a small piece of food would be delivered to their mouth on a spoon. Today Bessie is considered a genius—her invention was an early version of the feeding tube, which is essential in hospitals now.

Usha Mehta

Usha Mehta was sitting in a dark room speaking into a microphone. Everything she said could be heard on radios all across India. Suddenly the police started banging on the door. Usha was scared—it felt like her heart was pounding even louder than the banging on the door. But she kept talking. What had Usha done wrong?

Usha (pronounced OOH-sha) was born on March 25, 1920, in India. At the time, India was under British rule, but the British did not treat Indians fairly. They took most of the country's money and food, leaving everyone else poor and hungry. When Usha was five years old, she met a man who was wearing all white. He was very calm, and everyone treated him with respect. He was Mahatma Gandhi, and he would end up changing her whole life.

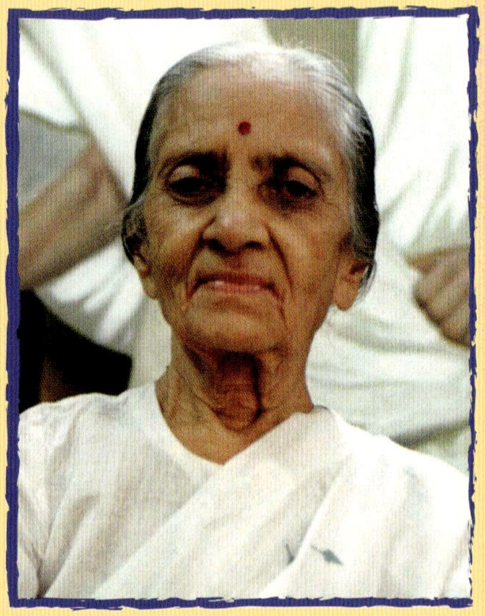

Mahatma believed that Indians should rule their own country. People agreed and reached for their weapons to fight the British. Mahatma stopped them. He said it would be better if they fought in peaceful ways, like marching and holding signs that explained how they felt.

When Usha grew up, she found her own peaceful way to join in. She started a secret club that would meet in a hidden place. They used a radio to share information with people all over the country about how badly the British were treating Indian people. They did this for two years until the police banged down the door and arrested Usha.

Usha was in jail for four years. But people remembered her messages and kept fighting. About a year after she was released, India won its independence from Britain!

Usha showed the world why speaking up is important.

A Look at India's History

India is a lively country—today it is known for dance, music, and festivals like Holi, which celebrates the coming of the spring season with vibrant powders that people throw onto each other.

Back in the 1600s, people from Britain traded with India for colorful fabrics, tasty spices, and tea. But then the British thought, why make trades when they could just take those things for themselves? The British started wars in India and eventually took control of the country. This is called colonialism. India wasn't the only country the British took over; they colonized countries all over the world.

For hundreds of years, the British took India's wealth and didn't share it with the Indian people who lived there. Beginning in 1858, they also ruled over India, and the Indian people didn't have a say. The Indians didn't regain control of their country until people like Mahatma and Usha fought back.

What Is an Obituary?

An obituary is a story in a newspaper about someone who has passed away. It tells us who they were, what they cared about, and how they made a difference. Obituaries also help us remember loved ones. When we read obituaries from a long time ago—even a century ago—we learn about history through real people's lives. And they remind us that everyone's story matters.

But not everyone's story has been told. For a long time, many newspapers mostly wrote about people who were rich, powerful, or famous. That meant a lot of amazing people—especially women, people of color, and people from the disability and LGBTQ communities—were left out. This book is trying to change that. It shares the stories of people who did big, brave, and creative things. Heroes whose stories have been hidden, until now.

Most newspapers have a team of writers who find out all they can about a person's life before typing out their story on a computer. They talk to family and friends, look at old photos and letters, and check for important dates and events—where the person grew up, what they loved to do, and how they changed the world. Sometimes newspapers even write obituaries ahead of time—especially for famous people—so they can share the story quickly when the time comes.

Obituaries usually include some helpful information that answers questions like: When was the person born? Who were their family and friends? Did they play sports or write poetry? The really good obituaries give an even fuller picture of what that person was like. What made them laugh? What made them cry? What made them different from other people?

People have been telling stories to remember others for a long, long time—at first on stone walls, then on paper made from plants, and now in newspapers and online. However we tell them, these stories help us remember. They help us learn. And they remind us that everyone has a story worth telling.

Give It a Try

Think about someone you've lost—maybe a family member, a neighbor, a pet, or even a famous person you admired. Try writing a few sentences about them. What made them special? What did they love to do? How did they make you feel?

You can also draw a picture to go with your story.

Remember: Writing about someone is a beautiful way to keep their memory alive.